THE
CARROT
COOKBOOK

BASIC INGREDIENTS

THE
CARROT
COOKBOOK

MORE THAN SIXTY
EASY, IMAGINATIVE RECIPES

EDITED BY
NICOLA HILL

COURAGE
BOOKS
AN IMPRINT OF
RUNNING PRESS BOOK PUBLISHERS

Philadelphia • London

Canadian representatives:
General Publishing Co., Ltd.,
30 Lesmill Road, Don Mills, Ontario M3B 2T6

10 9 8 7 6 5 4 3 2 1
Digit on the right indicates the number of this printing.
Library of Congress Cataloging-in-Publication number 94-73876
ISBN 1-56138-495-X

Printed in Singapore

Acknowledgements
Executive Art Editor: Penny Stock
Designer: Louise Leffler
Commissioning Editor: Nicola Hill
Editorial Assistant: Kathy Steer
U.S. Consultant: Liz Granirer
Production Controller: Melanie Frantz
Photographer: Jeremy Hopley
Home Economist: Annie Nichols
Stylist: Blake Minton
Illustrator: Marc Adams
Varieties text written by Dr. Peter Crisp of Innovar Plant Breeding

This edition published in the United States of America in 1995
by Courage Books, an imprint of
Running Press Book Publishers
125 South Twenty-Second Street
Philadelphia, Pennsylvania 19103-4399

CONTENTS

Notes

Microwave methods are based on microwave ovens with a High
Power output of 800 watts.

All the jellies, jams and preserves should be processed in a boiling
water-bath canner according to the USDA guidelines.

Storage notes: Cut off the leafy tops and store covered in a cool, dark,
dry place or in the refrigerator for 1-3 weeks. Do not freeze. Carrots
turn bitter if kept near apples.

Although they are a traditional crop, carrots owe much of their increasing popularity to the modern food industry. They are easy to grow, with high yields – but the real advantage is that they are brightly colored. Over the last few decades they have been used extensively in pre-prepared foodstuffs to add both bulk and color. Because there were ready markets for carrots in the food industry, commercial growers and breeders improved the crop, with corresponding benefits to the fresh market crop. Now, good-quality carrots are available throughout the year, and cooks need no longer regard carrots as just another "boiled root vegetable."

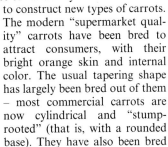

Originating in Afghanistan as purple and yellow rooted crops, carrots were introduced to northwestern Europe 600 years ago, and the orange type – originally named the Horn carrot – was developed in Holland in the mid-1700s. When the Horn carrot first appeared it was considered attractive enough to figure consistently in paintings by the Dutch Masters. Most modern carrot varieties throughout the world developed from this type. Indeed, the name Horn persists for what are now regarded as quite dissimilar kinds of carrot, as over the last two centuries the orange carrot diversified according to soils, climates, and tastes. Regional types developed which differed in root size and shape, in the time of season when the root swelled, and in their ability to be stored through the winter.

From the modern breeder's point of view, these different regional types represent a rich source of variability which can be used to construct new types of carrots. The modern "supermarket quality" carrots have been bred to attract consumers, with their bright orange skin and internal color. The usual tapering shape has largely been bred out of them – most commercial carrots are now cylindrical and "stump-rooted" (that is, with a rounded base). They have also been bred to suit commercial growers, with high yield and uniformity, and enough strength to withstand being harvested by machine. The breeders have managed these advances by recombining the characteristics of regional types from Europe, Japan, Australia and north Africa. Although carrots grown in Europe and the U.S. are still usually categorized as Amsterdam, Nantes, Paris Market and so on, in reality these usually reflect their shape rather than their origin.

Flavor

The flavor of carrots is partly due to their sugar content. Some varieties of "baby" carrots have been bred to have an increased sugar content when young. Usually, however, carrot sugars are higher in mature roots, especially if they have been growing in near zero temperatures for a few days.

The main "carroty" flavor is due to several compounds, such as petroselenic acid, typical of the plant family *Umbelliferae* to which carrots belong (as do parsnip, celery, and several highly flavored herbs – parsley, cilantro, etc.). The amounts of these compounds vary according to growing conditions, the age of the root, and to some extent, the variety. Generally, very young roots (baby carrots) make up in texture what they lack in flavor, and are suitable to be eaten raw. Full-grown carrots are available at their best in late summer and autumn, and can be eaten raw or cooked. Carrots which have been stored into or through the winter may need shredding to be eaten raw, and they may taste slightly peppery if they have been grown in wet soils; they are therefore probably best when cooked.

Color

The color of carrots has no effect on their flavor. However, the orange color is due to a nutritious class of compounds, usually termed carotenes, which form Vitamin A – vital in humans for normal growth, eye function and resistance to disease, and which may have anti-cancer properties.

The original orange carrots probably had fairly low levels of carotene, but breeders have improved carotene content –

Juwarot

partly by breeding varieties with orange rather than yellow cores. Indeed, during World War II the value of carrots as a source of carotene was recognized, and British breeders doubled the content of carotene in carrots in an attempt to improve the night vision of fighter pilots.

Modern varieties have even higher carotene levels, and current research makes it likely that varieties in a few years' time will have as much as five times more! The Juwarot variety – currently available in both the U.S. and Britain – is considered to have the highest carotene content.

Pesticides

Commercially grown carrots are usually treated with pesticides to prevent attack by insects, mainly the carrot fly. Because the carrot fly is active through much of the year, these pesticides need to remain active for weeks or months after they have been applied. Carrot growers know when these chemicals will have diminished to levels which are safe for consumers and there is a very large safety margin. However, if you are worried about pesticide residue in your carrots, whether bought or grown in the garden, peel them just before using them – virtually all of the pesticide remains in the outer tissues.

CARROT TYPES AND VARIETIES

The fortunes of carrots as a commercial crop have burgeoned, and breeding companies are producing dozens of new varieties each year. Nearly all of these varieties are high-quality F_1 hybrids. Most will be used by commercial growers for five years at most. After that, surplus seed tends to find its way into catalogs aimed at gardeners. Some of these varieties will be very good as amateur crops; however, their availability depends mainly on the "fallout" from commerce, and for that reason they are not discussed here. Instead, we concentrate on the characteristics of the main types of carrots, and most of the varieties we describe are not F_1 hybrids.

QUICK-MATURING

Amsterdam Forcing
This type matures 4-5 months after sowing to give small, tender "baby" carrots in early summer to early winter.

Amsterdam Forcing

The roots of these carrots are usually slender, cylindrical and stump-rooted, and are often sold tied in bunches with their foliage (which can be used as flavoring in soups). Unlike later-maturing types the young roots tend to develop a good deep orange color as soon as they start to swell.

The varieties of this type are usually identifiable by the prefixes "Am-," "Baby" or "Mini," or the name "finger;" other varieties include Sweetheart and Pampas.

Paris Market
Similar to the Amsterdam Forcing type in most respects, Paris Market carrots are readily recognizable because the roots are virtually spherical, 1¼-2 inches in diameter.

The type may have derived from the "French Early Short Horn," which was described a century ago as being "exclusively adapted for growing in vegetable mold." The traditional methods of growing high-quality, forced crops around Paris relied on copious amounts

Parmex

of animal and human manure being used to form hotbeds.

Carrots grown in highly manured soils are prone to produce forked roots, especially if they are long-rooted types. It seems likely that increasingly short types were developed to fit in with the Parisian growing methods. Because of its exceptional shape, Paris Market can be transplanted. Varieties often have the prefix "Par-" (e.g. Parabell, Pariska, Parmex), or have some reference to being round (e.g. Planet, Rondo, Golden Ball, Sweet Cherry Ball, Orbit). Other varieties include Kundulus, Thumbelina and Carpa.

Confusingly, the names Early French Frame and Early French Forcing can refer to the Amsterdam Forcing or Paris Market types.

MIDSEASON-MATURING

These are the typical fresh market carrots, available from midsummer until early winter.

Nantes
The type is cylindrical, stump-rooted, of medium size and usually classed as an early main

Panther

crop carrot. Much modern breeding has been based on the Nantes type, partly because in its traditional form it lacked the yellow core which typified most other kinds. Its widespread usage is responsible for the common perception today that tapered carrots are something of a novelty.

The Nantes type, because of its attractive features, is usually sold as a prepacked carrot. Modern (mostly F_1 hybrid) varieties of the Nantes type very

often have the prefix "Na-" or "Nan-" (e.g. Nairobi, Nantucket). Other varieties include the traditionally named Champion Scarlet Horn and Early Coreless as well as a plethora of other named varieties, the best known of which are probably Touchon, Panther, Tiptop and Sytan. The last variety has been found to be less susceptible to the carrot fly than others.

The Nantes type has been used extensively to breed improve-

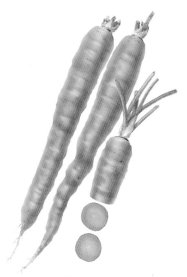

Centennial

ments into other kinds of carrots, and there are so-called "Baby Nantes" types, and sub-tropical varieties such as Nantes Mexican. The Nantes has also been used to develop sweet-tasting forcing varieties which are harvested like Amsterdam Forcing (e.g. Sucram, Suko, Sweet 'n' Short, Sweetheart), most are grown commercially for the restaurant trade rather than the fresh market.

Imperator
This type was developed in the U.S., is long and slightly tapered, and is mainly grown for the fresh markets.

Most varieties still carry the type name. Other varieties include El Presidente, Falcon, Centennial and Tendersweet.

Chantenay
The Chantenay (still sometimes called "Early Horn") is conical in shape, but with a rounded base. Its deep orange color adds to its appeal. Medium sized, of medium to late maturity, and with a good cooking quality, it is consistently crunchy rather than fibrous. This type is often grown for the fresh market; and has set the standard for com-mercially grown supermarket

varieties. It tends to have resis-tance to Alternaria disease.

Some varieties are prefixed "Red Cored -," and several have "Red" in their names (e.g. Redca, Long Red), but it is not exclusive to the Chantenay type.

Danvers
Similar to the Chantenay in most respects, except that the roots are tapered rather than stump-rooted. The very old vari-ety James Scarlet Intermediate (also known as English Horn) may be a Danvers type.

Red Cored Chantenay

Danvers

LATE-MATURING

Autumn King
This is the "traditional" type of carrot, being tapered and conical, sometimes with a stump root. It can grow to a very large size, is late in maturing, and is usually grown for the fresh market, often after storage in the field into winter.

Autumn King is a favorite with gardeners because it has a vigor-ous leaf, which helps suppress

Apart from those varieties named as Autumn King, the type includes Vita Longa, Campestra, Joba, Carovit, and the Australian variety Flakkee and its derivatives.

Berlicum
These carrots are cylindrical, stump-rooted, large, late-maturing, and give a heavy yield. The type was used extensively by the Campbell's Soups company to breed varieties suitable for their

Vita Longa

weeds. It also has some resistance to a virus disease (Carrot Motley Dwarf Virus, which causes leaves to be stunted and a purplish color, and reduces root size). This probably represents the main type of the otherwise apparently extinct English field carrots (Long Surrey, Long Horn, etc.) which, in contrast to the more delicate and finer quality French types, were grown as large, robust, coarse vegetables as fodder for domestic animals as well as for human consumption.

Camberley

canned soups, and several varieties have the prefix "Ca-" (e.g. Camberley, Cardinal). Other varieties include Oranza.

OBSCURE TYPES

Purple-Skinned Carrots
Purple-skinned (and sometimes, purple-fleshed) carrot varieties occasionally appear in American and European seed catalogues, usually with names such as "Afghan Black." The varieties currently available appear to have little to commend them as they tend to produce flowers rather than roots when grown in northerly latitudes, and few favorable comments have been made regarding their flavor.

Yellow and White Carrots
White and yellow carrot varieties are a traditional cattle fodder in northern Europe. Such varieties are usually available in seed catalogues as "Blanche (White) Belgian," "Blanche à Collet Vert," "White Vosges," "White French," and "Lobbericher." Some are very prone to greening on the exposed roots, and although this is considered a bad trait in orange carrots, greening of carrot roots is harmless (unlike potatoes!). There is evidence

Blanche (White) Belgian

that some of these white and yellow types may have resistance to the carrot fly. Aside from this, there is little reason to favor these varieties – they are generally described as bland, coarse, and susceptible to frost damage.

Oddly Shaped Carrots

Oddly shaped varieties are also sold. These include Oxheart (or Guerande), which has very short thick roots – like a Paris Market, but much larger; and St. Valery, a variety at least 100 years old, with very long tapering roots. The latter is much favored for horticultural exhibitions and attempts to grow carrots of record-breaking sizes.

St. Valery

CARROT FLY RESISTANCE

A new era in carrot breeding may be dawning as varieties are bred with resistance to the major pest of carrots – the carrot fly, whose maggots eat the roots. The first of these varieties, "Flyaway," appeared in seed catalogues in 1993, and several more should be released in the late 1990s.

Most have been bred from the variety Sytan and a German white fodder carrot, but some derive resistance from wild relatives of the carrot. The main advantage of these is that little or no pesticides will be needed. However, there may be a downside: insects tend to avoid plants which taste nasty; will the fly-resistant carrots taste as good to humans as the old varieties?

Flyaway

CARROT & LENTIL SOUP

Serves 4-6

1 tablespoon butter
1 onion, chopped
1 garlic clove, crushed (*optional*)
2 carrots, chopped
2 celery stalks, sliced
¾ cup red lentils, washed and drained
3½ cups vegetable stock
2 teaspoons lemon juice
about ½ cup milk
2 tablespoons chopped fresh parsley
salt and freshly ground black pepper
croutons, to serve (*see page 18*)

Melt the butter in a large saucepan and sauté the onion and garlic, if using, for 5 minutes, until soft. Add the carrots, celery and lentils and stir around in the butter for a few minutes. Pour in the stock, half cover, and simmer very gently for about 40 minutes, stirring occasionally.

Pour the soup into a blender or food processor and work until smooth, or rub through a strainer. Pour back into the cleaned pan and season to taste. Add the lemon juice and thin the soup with milk to the consistency you prefer. Stir in the parsley.

Serve the soup piping hot in individual bowls, sprinkling with croutons at the last moment.

CARROT & NOODLE SOUP

Serves 4-6

1 tablespoon corn oil
1 onion, chopped
1½ pounds carrots, finely chopped
1 teaspoon ground coriander
½ cup orange juice
3-3½ cups hot vegetable stock
1 cup dried egg noodles
3 tablespoons chopped fresh cilantro
salt and freshly ground black pepper
cracked peppercorns, for garnish

Heat the oil in a large saucepan and sauté the onion until soft. Add the carrots and ground coriander and cook for 5 minutes, stirring occasionally. Add the orange juice and 3 cups of the stock. Bring to a boil, lower the heat and simmer, partially covered, for 30 minutes.

Bring a saucepan of water to a boil. Add the noodles, stir and cover. Remove from the heat and leave for 6 minutes. Drain, then set aside.

Purée the soup in a blender or food processor, or rub through a strainer. Return to the cleaned pan and add the noodles. Stir in more stock if necessary. Add the cilantro, season and simmer until heated through. Serve garnished with cracked peppercorns.

Illustrated opposite

FRENCH CARROT BROTH

Serves 4-6
1½ tablespoons butter
5 ounces smoked bacon, diced
1½ pounds carrots, sliced
2½ cups water
2 zucchini, thinly sliced
1 can (*about 14 ounces*) white kidney
beans, drained
1 garlic clove, crushed
pinch of dried thyme
salt and freshly ground black pepper
1 tablespoon chopped fresh parsley,
for garnish

Melt the butter in a large saucepan. Add the bacon and carrots and cook for 4-5 minutes. Add the water and simmer gently, over a low heat, for about 15 minutes.

Add the zucchini, beans, garlic, thyme, and salt and pepper to taste. Cook over a low heat for a further 7-10 minutes, or until the vegetables are tender.

Sprinkle the soup with chopped parsley. Serve hot with crusty bread as a filling lunch or supper dish.

CURRIED CARROT SOUP

Serves 4-6
2 tablespoons butter
½ onion, sliced
1 garlic clove, chopped
¾ pound carrots, minced
2 cups chicken stock or water
½-inch piece of fresh ginger, minced
½ teaspoon curry powder
¼ teaspoon ground nutmeg
¼ teaspoon salt
½ cup light cream
freshly ground black pepper
1 tablespoon chopped fresh cilantro,
for garnish

Melt the butter in a large saucepan over a low heat. Add the onion and the garlic and sauté gently for a few minutes. Add the carrots, stir well, cover the pan and cook over a low heat for 10 minutes. Add the stock or water and bring to a boil.

Reduce the heat and add the ginger, curry powder, nutmeg and salt. Simmer for 30 minutes, then add the cream.

Place the soup in a blender or food processor and work until smooth, or rub through a strainer. Add pepper to taste. Serve the soup hot or chilled, garnished with the freshly chopped cilantro.

CHINESE CARROT & PORK SOUP

Serves 4-6

¼ **pound boned lean pork, very thinly sliced**
1 tablespoon soy sauce
1 tablespoon sesame seed oil
1 teaspoon cornstarch
½ **pound carrots, sliced**
4 cups chicken stock
2 teaspoons salt
chopped fresh cilantro, for garnish

Put the pork in a bowl with the soy sauce, sesame seed oil and cornstarch. Stir well, then cover and leave to marinate for 10 minutes.

Meanwhile, place the carrots, chicken stock and the salt in a saucepan, bring to a boil and simmer for 5 minutes. Add the marinated pork and simmer for 8-10 minutes, or until the pork and carrots are tender.

Pour into warmed soup bowls and sprinkle with chopped cilantro. Serve hot.

TOMATO & CARROT SOUP

Serves 4

1 can (*about 14 ounces*) chopped tomatoes
2 large carrots, minced
1 small onion, finely chopped
1 cup vegetable stock
1 teaspoon dried oregano
pinch of ground nutmeg
1 bay leaf
1 teaspoon brown sugar
salt
sprigs of parsley, for garnish

Place the chopped tomatoes and their juice in a saucepan. Add the carrots, onion, stock, oregano, nutmeg, bay leaf, sugar, and salt to taste. Bring to a boil, stirring continuously.

Reduce the heat, cover, and simmer for about 3 minutes. Remove and discard the bay leaf and pour the soup into a hot tureen. Serve garnished with parsley sprigs.

MICROWAVE METHOD: Place the tomatoes and juice, carrots, onion, boiling hot stock, oregano, nutmeg, bay leaf, sugar and salt in a casserole dish. Cover and cook on High for about 7-8 minutes. Serve as above.

VEGETABLES A LA GRECQUE

Serves 4

2 tablespoons olive oil
4 carrots, finely chopped
2 Spanish onions, finely chopped
½ cup dry white wine
1 bouquet garni
½ pound button mushrooms
8 tomatoes, peeled and seeded
salt and freshly ground black pepper
4 tablespoons chopped fresh parsley,
for garnish

Heat the oil in a saucepan and add the carrots and onions. Sauté until golden. Add the wine and the bouquet garni, and season to taste with salt and pepper.

Reduce the heat and add the mushrooms and tomatoes and a little more wine if necessary. (There should not be too much liquid as the mushrooms will add juice during cooking.) Cook, uncovered, for 15-20 minutes. Remove and discard the bouquet garni, and pour the vegetables into a bowl. Let cool, then refrigerate. Serve chilled, garnished with the chopped parsley.

CELERIAC & CARROT REMOULADE

Serves 4

1 celeriac root, about ½ pound, peeled
2 tablespoons lemon juice
½ pound carrots, cut into thin strips
salt
REMOULADE DRESSING:
4 tablespoons mayonnaise
½ cup thick yogurt
1 garlic clove, crushed
1 tablespoon chopped fresh parsley
1 tablespoon finely snipped fresh chives, plus
extra for garnish
½ teaspoon mustard powder
pinch of cayenne pepper, plus extra for garnish
1 hard-boiled egg, chopped, for garnish

Cut the celeriac into strips, dropping them into a bowl of water with 1 tablespoon lemon juice. Cook with the carrots and remaining lemon juice for 5-8 minutes. Drain and let cool. Mix the dressing ingredients and season. Toss the celeriac and carrots in the dressing, and garnish with chives, cayenne and egg.

MICROWAVE METHOD: Place the celeriac, carrots, a little lemon juice and 5 tablespoons water in a casserole dish. Cover and cook on High for 6-8 minutes. Finish as above.

Illustrated opposite

CARROT & COUSCOUS SALAD

Serves 4-6

1½ pounds couscous
2 large carrots, minced
½ red onion, finely chopped
½ cup mayonnaise
salt and freshly ground black pepper
red onion rings, for garnish

Place the couscous in a dish and moisten with warm water. Let stand for 10 minutes. Place the couscous in a strainer and steam over boiling water for about 15 minutes, or until soft. Let cool.

Place the cooked couscous, carrots and onion in a large bowl and stir well to mix. Add the mayonnaise and season with salt and pepper to taste. Toss gently to coat and mix thoroughly. Cover and chill until required.

Stir the salad before serving. Serve garnished with red onion rings.

CARROT & WATERCRESS SALAD

Serves 4

6 slices of white bread, crusts removed
2 tablespoons corn oil
½ stick butter
½ pound carrots, minced
2 bunches of watercress

DRESSING:

grated rind and juice of 1 orange
½ teaspoon sugar
1 garlic clove, crushed
4 tablespoons olive oil
salt and freshly ground black pepper

FOR GARNISH:

slices of orange
Danish blue cheese, crumbled

Cut the bread into small cubes. Heat the oil and butter together in a saucepan, add the bread cubes and cook until golden, stirring frequently. Drain on paper towels.

Gently mix the carrots and watercress. To make the dressing, place the orange rind and juice in a small bowl. Add the sugar, garlic, olive oil and seasoning to taste. Stir together well until emulsified, then pour over the carrot mixture and toss well. Sprinkle over the croutons and serve garnished with slices of orange and crumbled Danish blue cheese.

CARROT & WALNUT SALAD

Serves 4

1 pound carrots, coarsely minced
1 small onion, thinly sliced
2 tablespoons walnuts, coarsely chopped
⅓ cup golden raisins
2 tablespoons chopped fresh parsley, for garnish
DRESSING:
grated rind and juice of 1 orange
2 tablespoons lemon juice
3 tablespoons olive oil
1 garlic clove
¼ cup walnuts, coarsely chopped
salt and freshly ground black pepper

To make the dressing, put the orange rind and juice, lemon juice, olive oil, garlic and walnuts into a blender or food processor and work until smooth. Add salt and pepper to taste.

Place the carrots in a large bowl with the onion and mix together. Stir the dressing into the carrot mixture, together with the walnuts and the golden raisins. Sprinkle with the chopped parsley before serving.

FRUITY COLESLAW

Serves 6

½ cup plain yogurt
3 cups finely chopped white cabbage
2 large carrots, minced
2 green apples, quartered, cored and sliced
2 tablespoons lemon juice
⅔ cup seedless green grapes
½ cup pecans, coarsely chopped
2 tablespoons snipped fresh chives
salt and freshly ground black pepper

Place the yogurt in a large mixing bowl. Season to taste with salt and pepper. Stir in the cabbage and carrots.

Lightly toss the apple slices in the lemon juice and add to the cabbage mixture with the grapes, pecans and chives. Toss well so that all the ingredients are coated with the yogurt and serve.

MARINATED HERBED CARROTS

Serves 4

½ pound carrots, cut into 1½-inch thin strips
1 tablespoon sugar
about 1 tablespoon lemon juice (*optional*)
salt and freshly ground black pepper

DRESSING:

1 tablespoon tarragon vinegar
¼ teaspoon Dijon mustard
4 tablespoons olive oil
1 small garlic clove, crushed
1 tablespoon finely chopped fresh parsley
2 teaspoons finely snipped fresh chives
1 teaspoon chopped fresh thyme

Place the carrots in a saucepan. Add sugar, ½ teaspoon salt and enough water to cover. Bring to a boil and cook for 5 minutes.

To make the dressing, mix the vinegar and mustard in a bowl. Beat in oil, 1 tablespoon at a time, to make a creamy mixture. Stir in the garlic and herbs. Drain the hot carrots and mix with the dressing. Season, adding more sugar if you like. If you wish, sharpen the flavor with lemon juice. Chill before serving.

MICROWAVE METHOD: Place the carrots in a casserole dish with ½ teaspoon sugar, ½ teaspoon salt and 5 tablespoons water. Cover and cook on High for 4-5 minutes. Finish as above.

INDIAN-STYLE CARROTS

Serves 6

¼ cup butter
1½ pounds carrots, sliced
1 potato, peeled and diced
2 teaspoons ground cumin
½ teaspoon chili powder
1 teaspoon ground coriander
½ teaspoon turmeric
6 tablespoons water
1 teaspoon salt
small sprigs of fresh cilantro or parsley,
for garnish

Melt the butter in a large saucepan, add the carrots and potato and cook gently for about 5 minutes. Add the spices, measured water and the salt. Stir well, cover the saucepan and simmer for a further 7 minutes, or until the water has been absorbed.

Serve the carrots immediately, garnished with sprigs of fresh cilantro or parsley.

Illustrated opposite

POTATO & CARROT BOULANGERE

Serves 4

1 pound potatoes, thinly sliced
½ pound carrots, thinly sliced
1 small onion, thinly sliced into rings
2 ounces bacon slices, finely chopped
¾ cup Gruyère cheese, shredded
1 cup chicken stock
a little corn oil
salt and freshly ground black pepper

In a large casserole dish arrange the potatoes, carrots, onion, bacon and Gruyère, in alternate layers, seasoning the vegetable layers with salt and pepper, and finishing with a layer of potato.

Pour in the chicken stock. Cover the casserole dish and bake in a preheated oven, 400°F, for 30 minutes. Uncover, brush the top with corn oil and bake for a further 30 minutes, or until the potatoes are cooked and browned on top. Serve hot.

VICHY CARROTS

Serves 4

1 pound young carrots, thickly sliced
½ cup water
1 tablespoon butter
2 teaspoons sugar
salt
chopped fresh parsley, for garnish

Place the carrot slices in a large heavy-bottom saucepan with the measured water, butter and sugar. Cover the pan and cook for 5 minutes, or until the carrots are just tender.

Remove the lid, add a pinch of salt and continue cooking until all the liquid has evaporated, leaving the carrots coated with a syrupy glaze.

Serve the carrots hot, sprinkled generously with chopped parsley.

MICROWAVE METHOD: Place 3 tablespoons water, 1 teaspoon sugar and the carrots in a large bowl. Cover and cook on High for 6-9 minutes, or until tender, stirring halfway through cooking. Drain the liquid from the carrots and stir in ¼ stick butter until melted. Fold in the chopped fresh parsley and serve hot.

CARROTS HOLLANDAISE

Serves 4

1 pound long, thin carrots
a little water or chicken stock (*optional*)
½ stick butter
2 teaspoons sugar
2 egg yolks
3 tablespoons heavy cream
2 tablespoons finely chopped fresh parsley
salt and freshly ground black pepper

Steam the carrots or simmer them in a little salted boiling water or stock until they are barely tender. Put them in a strainer and pour cold water over them until they are cool enough to handle. Trim the carrots and rub off the skins. Cut them into 2-inch long pieces and then slice them thinly lengthwise.

Melt the butter in a pan. Mix in the carrots, sprinkling them with sugar. Cook over a very low heat, shaking the pan occasionally, until the carrots are tender. Beat the egg yolks with the cream. Mix in the parsley and seasoning.

Remove the carrots from the heat. Pour in the egg mixture and stir until thickened, to make a rich, creamy sauce. If necessary, return the pan to a low heat for about 1 minute to allow the sauce to thicken without curdling. Alternatively, stand the pan in a larger one of barely simmering water to finish the sauce. Serve immediately.

ORANGE GLAZED CARROTS

Serves 4

6 carrots, sliced
3 tablespoons orange juice
1½ tablespoons firmly packed brown sugar
½ stick butter or margarine
6 whole cloves
salt and freshly ground black pepper
strips of orange rind, for garnish

Cook the carrot slices in a small quantity of salted boiling water until they are just tender but still crisp. Drain and place in a serving dish; keep warm.

Put the orange juice, sugar, butter and cloves into a large saucepan, season with salt and pepper, and heat to simmering point. Remove the cloves with a slotted spoon and pour the sauce over the carrot strips. Leave for a few minutes before serving, garnished with strips of orange rind.

CHINESE CARROT & MUSHROOM STIR-FRY

Serves 4

2 tablespoons sesame seed oil
1¼ cups carrots, cut into thin strips
1 green pepper, cored, seeded and thinly sliced
½ pound mushrooms, sliced
1 can (*about 8 ounces*) bamboo shoots, drained
2 tablespoons light soy sauce
2 tablespoons hoisin sauce
2 tablespoons vegetable stock

Heat the oil in a wok or large heavy skillet. Add the carrots and green pepper and stir-fry for 1 minute.

Add the mushrooms and cook for 2 minutes, stirring occasionally. Add the bamboo shoots, then gradually stir in the soy sauce, hoisin sauce and vegetable stock. Bring to a boil, simmer for 1 minute, then serve immediately.

CARROTS WITH ALMONDS & GINGER

Serves 4

1 cup slivered almonds
2 tablespoons corn oil
1 onion, sliced
2-inch piece of fresh ginger, peeled and cut into thin strips
¾ pound young carrots, cut into thin strips
4 tablespoons vegetable stock or water
2 tablespoons sweet sherry
salt and freshly ground black pepper

Heat a wok or large skillet until hot. Add the almonds and dry-fry over a gentle heat, stirring frequently, until golden brown on all sides. Remove from the pan and set aside.

Add the oil to the pan and place over a moderate heat. When the oil is hot, add the onion and ginger and stir-fry for 2-3 minutes or until softened, taking care not to let them brown. Add the carrots, stock or water, sherry and salt and pepper to taste. Increase the heat to high and stir-fry for 3-4 minutes or until the carrots are just tender and the liquid has evaporated. Adjust the seasoning to taste and serve, sprinkled with the almonds.

Illustrated opposite

SWEET & SOUR CARROTS

Serves 4
4 tablespoons corn oil
½-inch piece of fresh ginger, peeled and
finely chopped
1 pound carrots, sliced
1½ cups water
2 tablespoons cider vinegar
1 tablespoon cornstarch
1 tablespoon firmly packed brown sugar
salt
fresh cilantro leaves, for garnish

Heat the oil in a skillet and cook the ginger for 1 minute, stirring constantly so that it does not brown. Add the carrots and stir-fry until all the pieces are coated with oil.

Add ½ cup of the water to the skillet and bring to a boil. Add salt to taste, cover and cook for 5-10 minutes, or until the carrots are just tender.

Meanwhile, blend the vinegar, cornstarch and sugar together until smooth and mix with the remaining water.

When the carrots are tender, remove the skillet from the heat and stir in the vinegar mixture. Return to the heat and stir until the sauce thickens and the carrots look glossy. Serve garnished with cilantro leaves.

BAKED LEMON CARROTS

Serves 4
2 tablespoons butter
1 tablespoon firmly packed brown sugar
1 tablespoon lemon juice
1 pound carrots, cut into evenly sized pieces
1 cup water
salt and freshly ground black pepper
2 teaspoons grated lemon rind, for garnish

Melt the butter in an ovenproof casserole dish, add the brown sugar and lemon juice, then add the carrots and stir them into the sugar and juice until they are well-coated.

Pour in the water, season with salt and pepper and bring to a boil. Cover the casserole dish and transfer to a preheated oven, 350°F. Cook for about 20-25 minutes, until the carrots are just tender.

Remove the casserole dish from the oven, return to the heat and bring to a boil, stirring gently until the liquid has evaporated and the carrots are coated with a buttery glaze. Serve the carrots immediately, sprinkled with the lemon rind.

PUREED CARROTS

Serves 4-6

2 pounds carrots, sliced
pinch of ground nutmeg
4 tablespoons butter
½ cup warm milk
1 egg yolk
1 tablespoon tomato paste
salt and freshly ground white pepper
finely snipped fresh chives, for garnish

Bring a large saucepan of lightly salted water to a boil. Add the carrots and the nutmeg. Bring back to a boil, lower the heat and cook gently for 20-25 minutes. Drain the carrots well and place in a blender or food processor with the butter, milk, egg yolk and tomato paste. Season with salt and pepper. Work to a smooth purée.

Return the carrot purée to the clean saucepan and place over a low heat until heated through and thickened slightly. Spoon the purée into a warmed serving dish and sprinkle with chives. Serve immediately.

MICROWAVE METHOD: Place the carrots in a large casserole dish with ½ cup of water. Add the nutmeg, cover and cook on High for 10-12 minutes or until tender. Drain and purée as above. Return to the casserole dish, cover and cook on High for 2-3 minutes, until slightly thickened, stirring 2-3 times. Garnish and serve as above.

VEGETABLE MEDLEY

Serves 4

1 pound carrots, cut into thin strips
¾ pound white turnips, cut into
½-inch cubes
½ pound shallots or baby onions, peeled
2 tablespoons butter
salt

BACON TOPPING:
1 onion, chopped
2 slices of bacon, cut into ½-inch squares
2 tablespoons butter
6 tablespoons fresh white bread crumbs
1 tablespoon chopped fresh parsley

Place the vegetables in the top of a steamer or a strainer that fits over a large saucepan. Sprinkle with salt and cover the pan. Steam over fast-boiling water for 12-15 minutes, until the vegetables are just tender.

Meanwhile, make the topping. Cook the onion and bacon in the butter for 4-5 minutes, stirring occasionally. Stir in the bread crumbs and cook for a further 2-3 minutes, or until they are golden brown. Stir in the parsley.

Toss the vegetables in the remaining butter and turn them into a serving dish. Sprinkle with the bacon topping and serve hot.

CARROT & ALMOND LOAF WITH TOMATO SAUCE

Serves 6-8

½ stick butter
1 onion, thinly sliced
2 garlic cloves, chopped
2 cups fresh whole wheat bread crumbs
½ pound carrots, minced
1¼ cups slivered almonds, toasted
2 eggs, beaten
4 tablespoons lemon juice
1 tablespoon chopped fresh parsley
1 teaspoon ground nutmeg
salt and freshly ground black pepper

TOMATO SAUCE:
2 tablespoons olive oil
1 onion, finely chopped
1 garlic clove, chopped
1 can (*about 14 ounces*) chopped tomatoes
2 tablespoons tomato paste
1 tablespoon chopped fresh basil

Melt the butter in a heavy skillet over a low heat and gently sauté the sliced onion and chopped garlic for about 5 minutes, or until just translucent but not brown.

Meanwhile, in a large bowl, combine the bread crumbs, carrots and almonds. Add the onion and garlic and stir well. Add the beaten eggs, lemon juice, parsley and nutmeg, season with salt and pepper and mix well. Add a little water if the mixture seems dry, then spoon the mixture into a greased 1-pound bread pan and bake in a preheated oven, 400°F, for about 45 minutes or until the loaf is nicely browned and a sharp knife inserted in the center comes out clean.

Towards the end of the cooking time, prepare the tomato sauce. Heat the oil in a skillet and sauté the onion and garlic for 5 minutes, or until just translucent. Add the tomatoes, tomato paste and basil and season with salt and pepper, stir well and simmer gently for about 10 minutes. Serve the loaf in slices with the hot tomato sauce.

MICROWAVE METHOD: Place the butter, onion and garlic in a large casserole dish and cook on High for 3 minutes. Stir in the bread crumbs, carrots and almonds. Add the eggs, lemon juice, parsley, nutmeg and seasoning. Spoon the mixture into an 8-inch x 5-inch microwave bread pan. Cook on High for 5 minutes, then on Medium for 8-10 minutes, until a knife inserted in the center comes out clean. Finish as above.

Illustrated opposite

CARROTS WITH ALMONDS & HORSERADISH

Serves 4

1 pound carrots, cut into thin strips
1 cup beef stock
½ stick butter
2 tablespoons all-purpose flour
2 egg yolks
½ cup heavy cream
2 tablespoons horseradish, minced
½ cup blanched almonds, chopped
salt and freshly ground white pepper

Simmer the carrots in the stock until just tender. Drain, reserving the stock.

Melt the butter in a saucepan and stir in the flour. Cook for 1-2 minutes, stirring. Add the reserved stock, season and bring to a boil, stirring. Mix the egg yolks with the cream and stir into the sauce. Remove from the heat and stir in the horseradish and almonds. Finally, fold in the carrots. Serve hot.

MICROWAVE METHOD: Place the carrots and hot stock in a casserole dish and cook on High for 8 minutes, or until just soft. Drain and reserve the stock. Place the butter in a jug and cook on High for 30-40 seconds. Stir in the flour, then gradually stir in the stock until thickened, stirring 2-3 times. Mix in the eggs and cream and finish as above.

CARROT & ZUCCHINI CUTLETS

Serves 4

¾ pound carrots, minced
¾ pound zucchini, minced
½ cup shredded Cheddar cheese
finely grated rind of ½ lemon
2 tablespoons chopped fresh parsley
1 tablespoon snipped fresh chives
2 tablespoons chopped nuts, toasted
6 tablespoons fresh whole wheat bread crumbs
1 egg plus 1 egg yolk, beaten
all-purpose flour, for dusting
beaten egg, for binding
1 cup almonds, chopped, for coating
2 tablespoons melted butter
salt and freshly ground black pepper

Mix together the carrots, zucchini, cheese, lemon rind, parsley, chives, toasted nuts, bread crumbs, egg and egg yolk, and season with salt and pepper. Work together until smooth. Shape into 8 small cutlets, using floured hands. Dip the cutlets into the beaten egg, then coat evenly with the chopped almonds. Chill for 1 hour.

Brush the cutlets on one side with melted butter; cook under a preheated broiler for about 5 minutes, then turn the cutlets over, brush the other side with butter and broil for a further 5 minutes. Serve hot.

VEGETABLE CURRY

Serves 4

3 carrots, thinly sliced diagonally
⅓ pound cauliflower flowerets, broken into
sprigs, with stalks sliced diagonally
¾ cup green beans, halved
¼ pound piece of white radish, peeled and
thinly sliced
2 tablespoons corn oil
1 small onion, finely chopped
1-inch piece of fresh ginger, peeled and
finely chopped
1 garlic clove, crushed
1 fresh chili, seeded and finely chopped
1 teaspoon hot chili powder, or according
to taste
½ cup water
3 tablespoons crunchy peanut butter
¾ cup frozen peas
salt
4 tablespoons dry roasted peanuts, chopped,
for garnish

Blanch the carrots, cauliflower, green beans and white radish separately in lightly salted boiling water, allowing 2 minutes for each type of vegetable. Drain, rinse immediately under cold running water and drain again.

Place a wok or large skillet over a moderate heat until hot. Add the oil and when the oil is hot, add the onion, ginger, garlic and chopped chili and stir-fry for 2-3 minutes, or until the onion is soft, taking care not to let the ingredients brown.

Add the chili powder and stir, mixing evenly, then add the measured water and peanut butter. Bring to a boil, stirring, then add the blanched vegetables, the frozen peas and salt to taste. Stir-fry for 3-4 minutes, or until all the vegetables are tender.

Serve the curry immediately, sprinkled with chopped dry roasted peanuts.

VEGETABLE SAMOSA PIE

Serves 6-8

2 tablespoons corn oil

1 onion, chopped

1 teaspoon cumin seeds

1 teaspoon mustard seeds

1 teaspoon chopped fresh ginger

¾ cup carrots, minced

2 cups potatoes, minced

¾ cup frozen peas

a handful of fresh cilantro leaves, chopped

2 tablespoons lemon juice

2 teaspoons curry powder

1 teaspoon ground coriander

¼ teaspoon chili powder

½ stick butter, melted

½ pound frozen filo dough, thawed

salt and freshly ground black pepper

Heat the oil in a skillet, add the onion, cumin and mustard seeds and ginger and cook for about 5 minutes, or until softened and lightly browned. Add the carrots and potatoes and cook gently for 6-8 minutes, until the vegetables are tender.

Add the frozen peas, chopped cilantro, lemon juice and spices. Season with salt and pepper and stir well. Cook for 5 minutes, stirring, then set aside.

Grease a 10-inch square baking sheet and have ready the filo dough, keeping the sheets of dough covered while you work to prevent them from drying out. Place 5-6 sheets of filo in the center of the baking sheet, turning each one at a slight angle to the one beneath to form a rough star shape, and brushing each with the melted butter. (The dough should overlap the edges of the baking sheet by about 4 inches. If your filo dough comes in smaller sheets, you can join pieces together, overlapping them by 1 inch.)

Put the vegetable filling in the center of the dough. Cover the filling with 3 more sheets of filo, brushing each with melted butter. Draw the bottom filo edges into the center to enclose the filling, then scrunch the dough on top and brush with the remaining butter.

Bake the pie in a preheated oven, 400°F, for about 25 minutes, or until the dough is golden brown and crisp. Serve the pie hot or cold, accompanied by green vegetables or a salad and a bowl of plain yogurt mixed with chopped fresh mint and cucumber.

Illustrated opposite and on page 3

SPICY ROOT VEGETABLE BRAID

Serves 6-8

½ stick butter, plus extra for greasing
1 onion, chopped
1 garlic clove, crushed
1 teaspoon minced fresh ginger
2 tablespoons chopped fresh thyme
1 potato, diced
2 carrots, diced
2 small parsnips, diced
1 tablespoon curry paste
2 tablespoons tomato paste
2 tablespoons mango chutney
½ cup vegetable stock
all-purpose flour, for dusting
2 packages (*about 1 pound*) puff pastry, thawed
if frozen
1 egg yolk
1 tablespoon milk
1 tablespoon sesame seeds

Melt the butter in a large heavy saucepan and sauté the onion, garlic, ginger and thyme for about 5 minutes. Add the vegetables and continue to cook for a further 10 minutes.

Stir in the curry paste, tomato paste, mango chutney and vegetable stock. Bring to a boil, cover and simmer gently for 15-20 minutes, until all the vegetables are just tender. Set aside to cool.

Meanwhile, roll out the puff pastry on a lightly floured surface to form an 11 x 15-inch rectangle. Transfer to a large greased baking sheet, cover with a clean dishcloth and set the pastry aside to rest while the vegetable filling is cooling.

Spoon the vegetable filling down the center third of the pastry. Using a sharp knife, cut slashes along each side of the filling at a slight angle, forming strips about 1-inch thick. Fold the strips alternately over the filling to make a braided effect, dampening them with a little water as you go. Press gently in the middle to seal in the filling.

Beat the egg yolk and milk together, brush over the braid and scatter over the sesame seeds. Bake in a preheated oven, 425°F, for about 20 minutes. Reduce the temperature to 375°F, and bake for a further 10 minutes. Serve the vegetable braid hot.

CHICKPEA & CARROT PIE

Serves 4-6

DOUGH:
1 cup whole wheat flour
1 cup all-purpose flour, plus extra for dusting
½ stick butter or margarine
¼ cup water
beaten egg, to glaze

FILLING:
2 tablespoons corn oil
1 onion, chopped
1 garlic clove, chopped
1 teaspoon chopped fresh ginger
1 teaspoon mustard seeds
1 teaspoon cumin seeds
4 carrots, minced
1½ cups potato, minced
1 teaspoon turmeric
½ teaspoon chili powder
½ cup thick coconut milk
¼ cup water
juice of 1 lime
1 can (*about 14 ounces*) chickpeas or butter
beans, drained
salt and freshly ground black pepper

To make the filling, heat the oil in a saucepan, add the onion and sauté for about 5 minutes, until softened and lightly browned. Stir in the garlic, ginger, mustard and cumin seeds and cook for a few minutes more. Stir in the carrots and potato, then reduce the heat, cover, and cook for about 5 minutes, or until the vegetables start to soften.

Stir in the turmeric and chili powder, then the coconut milk and water. Cover and cook gently for 5 minutes, then remove from the heat. Stir in the lime juice and chickpeas or butter beans, and season to taste. Let cool.

To make the dough, mix the flours together in a bowl. Season with salt and pepper. Heat the butter or margarine and water in a small saucepan until the butter has melted, then stir into the flour and mix quickly to a soft dough. Wrap tightly and leave to rest at room temperature for 15 minutes.

Roll out just over half the dough on a lightly floured surface and use to line an 8-inch pie pan, allowing the dough to overlap the edges. Fill with the cooked vegetable mixture. Roll out the remaining dough, dampen the edges of the filled pie and cover with the rolled out dough. Press the edges to seal, then trim off the surplus dough and pinch the edges together. Re-roll the trimmings and cut them into carrot shapes. Stick these on the top of the pie with beaten egg, then use more beaten egg to glaze the pie.

Bake the pie in a preheated oven, 400°F, for 35 minutes, until the dough is crisp and golden brown. Serve hot, accompanied by plain yogurt mixed with chopped fresh mint.

PASTA WITH GINGER & CARROT RIBBONS

Serves 4

**10 ounces dried pappardelle or other broad
egg noodles**
2 carrots, scrubbed
2 tablespoons butter
1-inch piece of fresh ginger, peeled and minced
2 tablespoons olive oil
2 tablespoons pine nuts, toasted
salt and coarsely ground black pepper

Bring at least 6 cups of lightly salted water to a boil in a large saucepan. Add a dash of oil and cook the pappardelle for 8-12 minutes, or according to the package directions, until it is just tender.

Meanwhile, using a potato peeler, pare the carrots to form flat ribbons. Melt the butter in a skillet and sauté the carrot ribbons and ginger for 5 minutes.

Drain the pasta well and return it to the clean pan. Toss with the olive oil and salt to taste. Carefully fold the carrot mixture into the cooked pasta. Sprinkle with the toasted pine nuts and coarsely ground black pepper and serve immediately.

Illustrated on front jacket

SPAGHETTI CARROTESE

Serves 4

12 ounces dried spaghetti
3 tablespoons olive oil
6 carrots, very thinly sliced
1½ cups tomatoes, peeled and chopped
3 tablespoons shredded fresh basil
salt and freshly ground black pepper

Bring at least 6 cups of lightly salted water to a boil in a large saucepan. Add a dash of oil and cook the spaghetti for 8-12 minutes, or according to the package directions, until it is just tender.

Meanwhile, heat the oil in a large skillet and cook the carrots over a high heat until just cooked, about 5-10 minutes. Add the chopped tomatoes and basil and season with salt and pepper to taste, mixing well.

Drain the pasta thoroughly and return it to the clean pan. Pour the carrot and tomato mixture over the spaghetti and toss well to combine. Serve immediately.

Illustrated opposite

ZUCCHINI & CARROT PANCAKES

Serves 4-6

PANCAKES:
1 cup whole wheat flour
½ teaspoon salt
1 egg
1 egg yolk
1 cup milk
corn oil, for cooking
½ cup sour cream, to serve
snipped fresh chives, for garnish

FILLING:
2 zucchini, minced
1 carrot, minced
8 tablespoons cream cheese, softened
2 tablespoons snipped fresh chives
salt and freshly ground black pepper

To make the pancake batter, combine the flour and salt in a bowl and make a well in the center. Add the egg and the egg yolk to the well and whisk, adding the milk a little at a time and gradually whisking in the flour. Whisk until smooth, then pour the batter into a jug and leave in the refrigerator for 1 hour.

Meanwhile, prepare the filling by combining all the ingredients in a bowl.

Heat a little oil in a small skillet. Pour in about 2 tablespoons of the pancake batter, quickly tipping the skillet so that the batter completely covers the bottom of the skillet. Cook gently until the underside is golden brown. Turn the pancake over and cook the other side for a few seconds. Place about 2 teaspoons of the vegetable filling in the center of the pancake, roll it up and transfer to a lightly greased ovenproof dish. Continue making and filling the pancakes in the same way until you have 12.

To serve, pour the sour cream over the pancakes, cover the dish tightly with foil and place in a preheated oven, 375°F, for about 10 minutes, until the pancakes are warmed through. Serve immediately, garnished with the chives.

CARROT & TAHINI PANCAKES

Serves 4-6

PANCAKES:

½ cup buckwheat flour or
whole wheat flour

½ cup all-purpose white flour

2 eggs, lightly beaten

3 tablespoons corn oil

½ cup milk

½ cup water

salt and freshly ground black pepper

FILLING:

1 tablespoon corn oil, plus extra
for brushing

1 teaspoon butter

½ cup cashews

1 pound carrots, coarsely shredded

1½ cups bean sprouts

1 tablespoon lemon juice

4 tablespoons light tahini

1 tablespoon chopped fresh parsley

To make the pancake batter, combine the flours, ½ teaspoon salt and a little pepper in a bowl and make a well in the center. Add the eggs, 1 tablespoon of the oil and half the milk to the well and mix to a smooth paste. Gradually whisk in the remaining milk and the water until smooth. Pour the batter into a jug and leave in the refrigerator for 1 hour.

Heat 1 teaspoon of the oil in a small skillet until it is smoking hot. Pour in about 2 tablespoons of the pancake batter, quickly tipping the skillet so that the batter completely covers the bottom of the skillet. Cook the pancake over a medium-high heat for about 2 minutes, then turn it over to cook the other side for about 1 minute.

Make 12 pancakes in this way, adding a little oil for each one. Keep them warm, layered between sheets of waxed paper, until they are all cooked.

To prepare the filling, heat the oil and butter in a skillet and gently cook the cashews for 2-3 minutes, until browned. Add the shredded carrots and cook for 3 minutes, stirring occasionally, then add the bean sprouts and cook for a further 3 minutes. Season with salt and pepper, add the lemon juice, then stir in the tahini and parsley. Spoon the filling onto the warm pancakes, roll them up and serve immediately.

CHICKEN & CARROT RICE

Serves 4

1½ cups basmati rice

1 teaspoon chili powder

3 skinless, boneless chicken breasts, cut
into strips

¾ stick of butter

2 garlic cloves, finely chopped

1 onion, sliced

⅓ cup almonds, halved

⅓ cup raisins

1 teaspoon turmeric

1 pound carrots, minced

1½ cups chicken stock

salt

sprigs of fresh cilantro, for garnish

Wash the basmati rice thoroughly under cold running water, then soak in plenty of cold water for about 30 minutes. Drain well.

Mix the chili powder and ½ teaspoon salt on a plate and lightly dip the chicken pieces in the mixture. Heat 2 tablespoons of the butter in a skillet, add the coated chicken strips and garlic and stir-fry for about 2 minutes.

Heat the remaining butter in a large saucepan, add the sliced onion, almonds and raisins and cook until golden and lightly browned. Stir in the turmeric, then the drained rice and cook, stirring, for 1-2 minutes. Season well with salt, then stir in the minced carrots, the chicken strips and the stock. Bring to a boil, cover the skillet with a tight-fitting lid, reduce the heat to very low and simmer for 20 minutes, or until the rice is cooked and all the liquid has been absorbed.

Transfer the chicken and carrot rice to a large, warmed serving dish and serve immediately, garnished with cilantro sprigs.

Illustrated opposite

SOMERSET CHICKEN WITH CARROTS

Serves 4
2 tablespoons corn oil
4 chicken pieces, skinned
1 tablespoon butter
2-3 celery stalks, coarsely sliced
1 large onion, coarsely chopped
2 tablespoons all-purpose flour
good pinch of mustard powder
1½ cups chicken stock
1½ cups dry cider or apple juice
1 pound carrots, thickly sliced
1 large bouquet garni
salt and freshly ground black pepper
chopped fresh thyme, for garnish

Heat the oil in a large ovenproof casserole dish or heavy saucepan, add the chicken and sauté over a moderate heat for 7-10 minutes, until golden on all sides. Remove the chicken with a slotted spoon and set aside on a plate.

Melt the butter in the casserole dish, add the celery and onion and cook over a gentle heat, stirring frequently, for about 5 minutes, until softened but not colored. Add the flour and mustard powder, stir well to mix with the celery and onion, then cook for 1-2 minutes, stirring constantly. Gradually stir in the stock and cider or apple juice and bring to a boil, stirring all the time. Add the carrots, bouquet garni and salt and pepper to taste, then return the chicken to the casserole dish with the juices that have collected on the plate.

Bring the liquid to a boil again, then cover the casserole dish and place in a preheated oven, 350°F, for 40 minutes, or until the chicken is tender when pierced in the thickest part with a skewer or fork. Turn the chicken pieces after 20 minutes, to ensure they are covered in liquid and cook evenly.

Remove and discard the bouquet garni. Adjust the seasoning to taste. Serve the casserole hot, garnished with chopped thyme, accompanied by plain boiled rice or creamy mashed potatoes.

MICROWAVE METHOD: Place the oil and chicken in a casserole dish. Cover and cook on High for 3 minutes. Rearrange after 2 minutes. Remove the chicken and set aside. Add the butter, celery and onion and cook on High for 3 minutes. Stir in the flour and mustard. Stir in 1 cup hot stock and 1 cup cider or apple juice. Cook on High for 3-4 minutes until thickened, stirring 2-3 times.

Add the carrots, bouquet garni, seasoning and chicken. Cover the dish and cook on High for 10 minutes. Reduce power to Medium and cook for a further 15 minutes. Serve as above.

VEAL & CARROT STEW

Serves 4

2 tablespoons corn oil
1½ pounds stewing veal, chopped
1 onion, chopped
1 teaspoon paprika
¾ pound carrots, cut into long thin strips
2 tomatoes, peeled and quartered
1 pickle, sliced
1 cup beef stock
salt and freshly ground black pepper

FOR GARNISH:
1 tablespoon chopped fresh parsley
pinch of cayenne pepper

Heat the oil in an ovenproof casserole dish or heavy saucepan, add the veal and onion and sauté until lightly browned. Season with salt and pepper, add the paprika and cook for about 5 minutes, stirring frequently.

Add the carrots, tomatoes and pickle to the casserole dish and cook for a further 4-5 minutes. Add the stock and enough hot water to cover the vegetables. Cover the pan and cook over a low heat for about 1½-1¾ hours, stirring occasionally.

Sprinkle the stew with parsley and cayenne pepper and serve with boiled baby potatoes or buttered noodles.

CARROT BURGERS

Serves 4

½ pound extra lean chopped beef or pork
½ cup fresh white bread crumbs
1 egg, beaten
1 tablespoon all-purpose flour, plus extra for dusting
pinch of ground nutmeg
½ pound carrots, finely minced
2 tablespoons corn oil (*optional*)
salt and freshly ground black pepper

Mix the meat with the bread crumbs, beaten egg and flour and season well with salt, pepper and nutmeg. Add the carrots and mix together well.

Divide the mixture into 8 portions with lightly floured hands and form into flat burger shapes. Heat the oil in a large skillet and cook the burgers over a medium heat, turning once or twice, for 10-15 minutes or until cooked through. Alternatively, cook the burgers under a preheated hot broiler. Serve hot in burger buns with sliced tomatoes, onions and crisp, shredded lettuce.

LAMB RAGOUT WITH SPRING VEGETABLES

Serves 4-6

2 pound boned shoulder of lamb, or lamb fillet,
trimmed of excess fat and cut into
2-inch cubes
½ cup all-purpose flour
2 tablespoons corn oil
½ stick butter
½ pound baby carrots, scrubbed
½ pound baby turnips, peeled
½ pound button onions, peeled and
left whole
1 garlic clove, crushed
1½ cups chicken stock
2 teaspoons tomato paste
small sprig of rosemary
¾ cup frozen peas
salt and freshly ground black pepper

Toss the meat in the flour seasoned with salt and pepper; shake off and reserve any excess flour. Heat the oil in a large ovenproof casserole dish or a heavy saucepan and cook the meat briskly on all sides, then remove from the dish and reserve.

Add the butter, the baby carrots, baby turnips, button onions and the crushed garlic to the casserole dish and cook gently until they are golden and lightly browned. Sprinkle in any leftover flour and cook gently, stirring, for about 1 minute. Gradually stir in the chicken stock, tomato paste and rosemary, and season with salt and pepper.

Bring to a boil, stirring constantly until the sauce has thickened and is smooth, then return the meat to the casserole dish.

Cover, reduce the heat and simmer, stirring occasionally, for 1 hour. Add the frozen peas and continue cooking for another 30 minutes, or until the meat is tender. Serve the lamb ragout immediately, with baked potatoes and a green vegetable.

Illustrated opposite

ORIENTAL BEEF & CARROT STEW

Serves 4

2 tablespoons corn oil
1 garlic clove, crushed
small piece of fresh ginger, peeled and chopped
1 shallot, chopped
1½ pounds stewing beef, cut into ½-inch cubes
3 tablespoons soy sauce
1 tablespoon sugar
1 tablespoon rice wine or sherry
½ teaspoon five spice powder
1 pound carrots, sliced diagonally

Heat the oil in a large casserole dish. Add the garlic, ginger and shallot and cook, stirring until golden brown. Add the beef and the remaining ingredients, except the carrots. Add just enough cold water to cover. Bring to a boil, cover, lower the heat and simmer for about 1½ hours. Add the carrots to the stew and simmer for a further 30 minutes, or until tender. Serve hot with mashed potatoes.

MICROWAVE METHOD: Place the oil in a casserole dish and cook on High for 30 seconds. Add the garlic, ginger and shallot and cook on High for 1 minute. Add the beef and remaining ingredients, except the carrots. Add 1½ cups of boiling water and cook on High for 10 minutes. Reduce power to Medium-Low for 1 hour. Add the carrots and cook on Medium for 20 minutes, then serve.

SPICY LENTIL, LEEK & CARROT STEW

Serves 4

1 large onion, chopped
2 tablespoons olive oil
½ pound leeks, sliced
½ pound carrots, diced
2 garlic cloves, crushed
1 tablespoon white mustard seeds
1 tablespoon coriander seeds
1 teaspoon turmeric
small piece of fresh ginger, peeled and minced
1⅓ cups split red lentils, washed and drained
3 cups water
1 tablespoon lemon juice
salt and freshly ground black pepper
chopped fresh cilantro, for garnish

Gently sauté the onion in the oil for about 5 minutes, then add the leeks and carrots, stir well and cook for a further 5 minutes. Add the garlic, mustard and cilantro seeds, turmeric, ginger and lentils and stir for 2-3 minutes. Then pour in the measured water.

Bring to a boil, then partially cover the saucepan, reduce the heat and leave the stew to simmer gently for 25-30 minutes, until the lentils are tender. Add the lemon juice and season to taste. Serve sprinkled with the chopped cilantro, accompanied by mango chutney and a salad of tomatoes and onions.

COUSCOUS WITH SPICED CARROT STEW

Serves 4

1¾ cups couscous
½ teaspoon salt dissolved in 2 cups warm water
2 tablespoons olive oil
2 tablespoons chopped fresh parsley

STEW:

2 tablespoons olive oil
2 onions, chopped
1 pound carrots, sliced
2 teaspoons ground cinnamon
2 teaspoons ground cumin
2 teaspoons ground coriander
⅔ cup raisins
2 cans chickpeas (*14 ounces each*), drained,
or 1 pound frozen broad beans, peas
or sweet corn
3 cups water
4 tablespoons tomato paste
salt and freshly ground black pepper
lemon wedges, for garnish

Place the couscous in a large bowl. Add the measured salted water and set aside.

Meanwhile, prepare the stew. Heat the oil in a large saucepan or the saucepan part of a steamer. Add the onions and carrots and cook for 10 minutes. Add the spices and cook for 2-3 minutes, stirring. Add the raisins and the chickpeas, beans, peas or sweet corn, the water and the tomato paste, and season with salt and pepper. Bring to a boil, then reduce the heat so that the stew just simmers.

By this time the couscous will have absorbed the water. Put the couscous into the top part of a steamer or a metal strainer, breaking it up a little with your fingers as you do so. Place the couscous over the stew, cover and steam for 25-30 minutes. Stir the olive oil and chopped parsley into the couscous and serve immediately, with the hot stew. Garnish with lemon wedges.

BAKED CARROT DESSERT

Serves 4-6

4 eggs
½ cup sugar
1¼ cups finely minced carrot
½ cup dried bread crumbs
4 tablespoons ground almonds
¾ teaspoon ground cinnamon
½ teaspoon ground nutmeg
¼ teaspoon salt
1 teaspoon vanilla extract
3 tablespoons melted butter
¾ cup raisins, dusted with
2 teaspoons flour
carrot ribbons, to decorate

Beat the eggs in a large mixing bowl until pale and doubled in volume, adding the sugar a little at a time. Fold in the carrot, bread crumbs and ground almonds, together with the spices, salt and vanilla extract. Stir in the melted butter and raisins.

Pour the mixture into a well-greased 3½ pint heatproof baking dish. Place the dish in a roasting pan of hot water and bake in a preheated oven, 350°F, for about 55 minutes or until the dessert is completely cooked in the center. (A skewer inserted in the middle should come out clean.) Turn out, decorate with carrot ribbons and serve warm with custard sauce.

CARROT & APPLE SOUFFLE

Serves 4

½ stick butter
¼ cup all-purpose flour, sifted
½ cup light cream
½ teaspoon ground cinnamon
2 tablespoons fresh white bread crumbs
4 eggs, separated
½ pound carrots, finely minced
½ pound dessert apples, peeled, cored
and shredded
½ cup walnuts, chopped

Melt the butter in a saucepan and stir in the flour to make a smooth paste. Add the cream and cinnamon and cook over a low heat until the sauce thickens. Cool slightly, then add the bread crumbs, egg yolks, carrots and apples.

Whisk the egg whites until stiff but not dry, then carefully fold into the mixture.

Pour into greased individual soufflé dishes. Sprinkle over the chopped walnuts and bake in a preheated oven, 400°F, for 15-20 minutes, until well risen and golden brown. Serve the soufflés immediately.

Illustrated opposite

GRANDMA'S CHRISTMAS PUDDINGS

Serves 8 from a large baking dish, or 4 from a small baking dish

1½ cups golden raisins

1½ cups currants

2¾ cups seedless raisins

¼ cup dried candied citrus peel

½ cup glacé cherries

⅔ cup chopped almonds

¾ cup ground almonds

1 cup fresh brown or white bread crumbs

2 carrots, minced

1 cooking apple, peeled, cored and shredded

½ teaspoon apple pie spice

pinch of ground nutmeg

½ teaspoon ground cinnamon

1 cup soft brown sugar

grated rind and juice of 1 large lemon

grated rind and juice of 1 orange

1 cup light corn syrup

4 eggs, beaten

4 tablespoons brandy

½ cup dark beer

1 cup vegetable shortening

butter, for greasing

Place all the ingredients in a large bowl, cut in the shortening, and stir well to mix.

Grease 3 4-cup heatproof baking dishes or 6 2-cup baking dishes well with butter. Fill each dish just over three-quarters full, then cover with greased waxed paper and foil or a pudding cloth. Tie securely with string.

Place each pudding in a saucepan and pour in boiling water to come halfway up the sides. Boil for 6-8 hours, depending on the size. Top off with more boiling water as necessary. Remove the puddings from the saucepans and leave overnight to cool completely.

Remove the coverings and cover again with fresh greased waxed paper and foil or a pudding cloth. Store in a cool, dry place away from direct sunlight. These puddings are very moist and will keep well for up to 2 years.

To serve, reboil for 3-4 hours, depending on the size, then turn out onto a warm dish. To ignite the pudding, warm 3-4 tablespoons of brandy in a ladle, pour over the pudding and set alight with a lighted taper. If decorating with a piece of holly on top, wrap the stem in a small piece of foil. Serve with brandy butter or cream.

MOIST CARROT & WALNUT CAKE

Makes a 7-inch round cake
1 cup firmly packed light brown sugar
¾ cup corn oil
2 eggs
1 cup whole wheat flour
1 teaspoon ground cinnamon
1 teaspoon baking soda
¾ cup coarsely minced carrot
½ cup walnuts, chopped

TOPPING:
2 tablespoons apricot jam, sieved
1 tablespoon lemon juice
½ cup walnuts, chopped

Line a 7-inch round cake pan with nonstick baking paper or greased waxed paper. (Use a fixed-base pan as the mixture is almost a pouring consistency.)

Put the sugar into a mixing bowl and, using an electric whisk, gradually whisk in the oil, then whisk in the eggs one at a time.

Mix together the flour, cinnamon and baking soda and stir into the oil and egg mixture, then add the minced carrot and chopped walnuts. Beat all the ingredients together with a wooden spoon until well combined, then pour the mixture into the prepared cake pan.

Place the cake in the center of a preheated oven, 350°F, and bake for about 1 hour and 10 minutes, or until the cake is risen and firm to the touch. Remove from the oven, leave to stand in the pan for 2-3 minutes, then turn out onto a wire rack, peel off the paper and let cool.

To make the topping, boil the apricot jam and lemon juice together in a small saucepan for 2-3 minutes. Brush the mixture generously over the top of the cooled cake and sprinkle the walnuts over immediately, as the glaze will set very quickly.

CARROT HALVA

Serves 4

1 pound carrots, minced
2½ cups milk
8 cardamom pods
5 tablespoons vegetable oil or clarified butter
5 tablespoons sugar
1-2 tablespoons golden raisins
1 tablespoon shelled, unsalted pistachio nuts,
lightly crushed
1 cup clotted or heavy cream,
to serve (*optional*)

Put the minced carrots, milk and cardamom pods in a heavy-bottom saucepan and bring to a boil. Reduce the heat to medium and cook, stirring occasionally, for about 1 hour, or until the milk has reduced by half.

Heat the oil or clarified butter in a nonstick skillet. When it is hot, add the carrot mixture. Stir and cook for about 10-15 minutes, until the carrots no longer have a wet, milky look. They should turn a rich, reddish color.

Add the sugar, golden raisins and pistachios. Stir and cook for another 2 minutes. Serve warm or at room temperature with the cream, if using.

SWISS HAZELNUT & CARROT CAKE

Makes a 7-inch square cake

3 large eggs, separated
½ cup sugar
¾ cup minced carrots
¾ cup hazelnuts, very finely chopped
2 teaspoons finely grated lemon rind
½ cup all-purpose flour
½ teaspoon baking powder

Well grease a 7-inch square cake pan.

Whisk the egg yolks with the sugar until thick and creamy. Stir in the carrots, hazelnuts and lemon rind. Sieve in the flour and baking powder and fold it in. Whisk the egg whites until they form stiff peaks, then carefully fold into the mixture.

Turn the mixture into the prepared cake pan and bake in a preheated oven, 350°F, for 40-45 minutes, until the cake is just firm to the touch. Let stand in the pan for about 2-3 minutes, then turn the cake out onto a wire rack to cool.

Illustrated opposite

CHRISTMAS CARROT CAKE

Makes an 8-inch round cake

1 cup golden raisins
4 tablespoons whiskey
1 cup corn oil
½ cup unrefined molasses
3 large eggs
1 tablespoon unsweetened cocoa powder
2 cups whole wheat flour
1 teaspoon ground cinnamon
½ teaspoon ground nutmeg
½ teaspoon ground allspice
½ teaspoon salt
1½ teaspoons baking powder
1½ teaspoons baking soda
1½ cups carrots, finely minced
1 cup walnuts, finely chopped

FROSTING:
¾ pound low-fat cream cheese
½ cup confectioner's sugar, sifted
finely grated rind of ½ lemon

Place the golden raisins in a bowl, pour over the whiskey and leave to soak for 1 hour.

Line a loose-bottomed 8-inch round cake pan with nonstick baking paper, or greased and floured waxed paper.

Beat together the oil and molasses, beating in the eggs one at a time. (At this stage the mixture looks very odd, but don't worry.) Still beating, add the cocoa powder, flour, spices, salt, baking powder and baking soda.

Mix in the minced carrots, the whiskey-soaked golden raisins and any remaining whiskey and the walnuts. Stir together well and tip the mixture into the prepared cake pan.

Bake in a preheated oven, 350°F, for about 1¼ hours; a warmed skewer inserted into the center of the cake will come out clean when the cake is cooked. Allow the cake to cool in the pan.

Place the cream cheese in a bowl and gradually work the confectioner's sugar into it. Add the lemon rind. When the cake is quite cold, spread the frosting over the top.

CARROT FRUITCAKE

Makes a 9-inch round cake

½ cup firmly packed brown sugar

6 tablespoons clear honey

1 cup carrots, finely minced

⅔ cup seedless raisins

⅓ cup pitted dates, chopped

½ teaspoon ground nutmeg

1 stick butter or margarine

½ cup water

1 egg, beaten

1 cup all-purpose white flour, sifted

1 cup whole wheat flour

2 teaspoons baking powder

TOPPING:

1 cup cream cheese, softened

2 tablespoons clear honey

1 teaspoon lemon juice

1 tablespoon chopped walnuts

Mix together the sugar, honey, carrots, raisins, dates, nutmeg, butter or margarine and water in a saucepan. Bring to a boil. Reduce the heat and simmer gently for 5 minutes. Turn into a mixing bowl and leave until cold.

Beat in the egg. Mix together the flours and baking powder and fold into the fruit mixture until thoroughly combined.

Lightly oil a 9-inch round cake pan. Line with nonstick waxed paper. Turn the mixture into the prepared tin and level the surface. Bake in a preheated oven, 350°F, for 55-60 minutes, or until firm to the touch. Cool on a wire rack.

Beat together the cream cheese, honey and lemon juice. Spread evenly over the surface of the cooled cake and sprinkle over the walnuts.

CARROT & BANANA BREAD

Makes a 1-pound loaf
2 cups all-purpose flour
½ teaspoon salt
1 teaspoon baking powder
1 stick butter
½ cup firmly packed brown sugar
1 ripe banana, mashed
2 carrots, minced
2 eggs, beaten

Sift the flour, salt and baking powder together into a large bowl. Rub in the butter with your fingertips until the mixture resembles fine bread crumbs. Add the brown sugar.

Combine the mashed banana with the minced carrots and beaten egg and add to the flour mixture. Mix together well, but do not overmix as this will make the texture heavy.

Pour the mixture into a well-greased 1-pound bread pan and bake in a preheated oven, 400°F, for 1 hour or until a warmed skewer inserted in the center comes out clean. Allow the bread to cool in the pan. Serve sliced, with or without butter.

CARROT HEART COOKIES

Makes 8 large cookies
⅔ cup all-purpose flour, plus extra for dusting
¾ stick butter or block margarine, at room temperature
1 egg yolk
½ cup carrots, finely minced
sugar or confectioner's sugar, for sprinkling

Sift the flour into a bowl, and then rub in the butter or margarine, using your fingertips, until the mixture resembles fine bread crumbs. Add the egg yolk and carrots and work together, using your hands, to make a smooth dough.

Roll out the dough quite thinly on a lightly floured surface and cut out the cookies using a heart-shaped cutter. Lightly knead any trimmings together and re-roll.

Place the cookies on a lightly greased baking sheet and bake in a preheated oven, 375°F, for 25-30 minutes, until golden brown. Sprinkle the sugar over the cookies while they are still hot.

Illustrated opposite

COCONUT & PECAN CARROT CAKE

Serves 10-12

1¾ cups all-purpose flour, plus 2 tablespoons
for coating
½ teaspoon salt
1 teaspoon baking soda
1½ teaspoons baking powder
½ teaspoon ground cinnamon
¼ teaspoon grated nutmeg
3 eggs
1 cup sugar
¾ cup corn oil
2¼ cups finely minced carrots
2 teaspoons shredded orange rind
2 tablespoons unsweetened dehydrated coconut
½ cup pecans, chopped
⅔ cup raisins or golden raisins
10-12 pecan halves, to decorate

FROSTING:
1 egg
½ cup light cream
1 cup confectioner's sugar, sifted
½ stick butter
1½ cups unsweetened dehydrated coconut
½ cup pecans, chopped

Sift together the flour with the salt, baking soda, baking powder and spices and set aside.

Beat the eggs with an electric mixer, gradually adding the sugar, and beating until the mixture is thick and pale. Slowly pour in the oil, beating constantly until it is completely absorbed, then fold in the flour mixture, a third at a time.

Toss the carrots, orange rind, dehydrated coconut, pecans and raisins or golden raisins with the remaining flour, then stir into the cake mixture. Pour into a greased 7 x 11-inch or 8 x 12-inch pan. Bake in a preheated oven, 350°F, for about 45 minutes, until a warmed skewer inserted in the center comes out clean. Let cool in the pan.

Meanwhile, make the frosting. Beat the egg and cream together with the sugar. Place in a saucepan with the butter and cook over a moderate heat, stirring constantly, for about 7-8 minutes, until thickened. Remove from the heat and stir in the dehydrated coconut and pecans. Set aside to cool.

Spread the cooled frosting over the cake. Cut into squares, place a pecan half on each square and serve.

CARROT JUICE

Makes 4 small glasses
1 pound carrots, finely minced
¼ cup sugar
4 tablespoons lemon juice
2 cups cold water

Place the carrots in a bowl and sprinkle with the sugar and lemon juice; let stand in a cool place for a few minutes.

Add the measured water, stir well and let stand for 1 hour.

Pass the carrot juice through a strainer and chill until required. Serve the juice as it is or use as a basis for Carrot Flip (see right).

CARROT FLIP

Makes 4 small glasses
1 cup carrot juice *(see left)*
1 cup light cream
4 egg yolks
½ cup fresh orange juice
crushed ice
thin slices of orange, to decorate

Put the carrot juice, cream, egg yolks and orange juice into a cocktail shaker and mix well. Alternatively, place the ingredients in a bowl and whisk to combine thoroughly.

Pour into tall glasses containing crushed ice and serve immediately, decorated with slices of orange.

Illustrated on page 1

CARROT RAITA

Makes about 1 cup

2 young carrots, minced
1 tablespoon minced onion
1 cup plain yogurt
2 tablespoons olive oil
1 teaspoon orange juice
1 teaspoon ground coriander
½ teaspoon cumin seeds, crushed
2 teaspoons finely chopped fresh dill
pinch of ground cardamom
salt and freshly ground black pepper

Put the minced carrots in a large bowl, add the minced onion and stir together. Add all the remaining ingredients, season to taste and mix thoroughly until well-blended.

Cover the bowl with plastic wrap and chill in the refrigerator for about 30 minutes.

Serve the chilled raita with broiled meat or oily fish such as mackerel.

CARROT & ORANGE CHUTNEY

Makes about 2-3 pounds

¾ pound carrots, minced
½ pound onions, thinly sliced
½ pound cooking apples, peeled, cored and shredded
¾ cup firmly packed brown sugar
⅓ cup raisins
2 whole cloves
shredded rind and juice of 4 oranges
1½ cups cider vinegar

Place the carrots, onions and apples together in a large saucepan with the sugar, raisins, cloves and shredded rind and juice of the oranges. Pour over the vinegar.

Bring to a boil, then reduce the heat, cover and simmer for 40 minutes. Remove the lid and simmer for a further 40 minutes, until the chutney is fairly thick.

Meanwhile, sterilize and have ready warmed jars. Pour the chutney into the jars, leave for a few minutes, and then cover tightly and label. Serve with cold meats, poultry, or bread and cheese.

Illustrated opposite

SPICY MIXED VEGETABLE RELISH

Makes about 3 pounds
½ pound eggplants, halved lengthwise
⅓ pound onion, minced
½ pound carrot, minced
½ pound tiny cauliflower flowerets
1½ tablespoons salt
1½ cups cider vinegar
½ cup water
¾ cup firmly packed dark brown sugar
1 teaspoon cilantro seeds
½ teaspoon ground ginger
1½ teaspoons curry powder
1 tablespoon pickling spice, tied in cheesecloth
¾ cup frozen sweet corn
¾ cup frozen peas
1 tablespoon slivered almonds
1 tablespoon cornstarch
2 tablespoons water

Cut the eggplants into very thin slices. Put into a large bowl with the minced onion and carrot, and the cauliflower flowerets. Sprinkle the salt over the vegetables. Pour in enough water just to cover the vegetables and let stand overnight.

Next day, drain the vegetables well and squeeze with your hands to extract as much water as possible.

Put the vinegar, measured water, sugar and all of the spices in a saucepan, bring to a boil, then lower the heat and simmer for about 20 minutes.

Add the drained vegetables, sweet corn, peas and almonds to the pan, cover, and simmer for 10 minutes. Remove the lid and boil fast for about 7 minutes, then remove the cheesecloth bag of pickling spice.

Blend the cornstarch and water together until smooth and stir into the pan. Boil the relish for a further 3 minutes, stirring until it is thickened. Pour into warmed sterilized jars, seal and label. Serve with broiled or cold meat or poultry.

CARROT & ORANGE MARMALADE

Makes about 5½ pounds
1½ pounds oranges, thoroughly washed and halved
4 cups water
2 pounds carrots
2 pounds sugar

Squeeze the juice from the oranges and reserve. Collect all the seeds and tie in a piece of cheesecloth. Cut up the peel fairly coarsely and place it, with the juice and the bag of seeds, in a large bowl. Pour over the measured water, cover the basin and leave overnight.

Next day, place the orange mixture in a large pan, bring to a boil, then reduce the heat and simmer gently until the peel is quite tender and the weight of the pulp is 2½ pounds. Remove and discard the bag of seeds.

Cook the carrots in 2 cups of water in a covered saucepan until tender. Drain the carrots, reserving the cooking water, then purée the carrots in a blender or food processor, or rub through a strainer.

Add the carrot purée and the reserved cooking water to the orange mixture, bring to a boil, add the sugar and boil rapidly for about 1 hour, until it has a fairly thick consistency.

As this marmalade contains little sugar it will not keep longer than a week or so unless hermetically sealed. This may be done by pouring the marmalade into hot sterilized jars and sealing with waxed discs, placed wax-side down. The covered jars should then be immersed while hot in a pan of hot water, brought to a boil, and boiled for 5 minutes. The marmalade will then keep for months.

Illustrated on pages 2-3

THE
CARROT
INDEX